Spill

BRUCÉ SMITH

Spill

THE UNIVERSITY OF CHICAGO PRESS
Chicago & London

The University of Chicago Press, Chicago 60637
The University of Chicago Press, Ltd., London
© 2018 by The University of Chicago.
Published 2018
Printed in the United States of America

27 26 25 24 23 22 21 20 19 18   1 2 3 4 5

ISBN-13: 978-0-226-57041-9 (paper)
ISBN-13: 978-0-226-57055-6 (e-book)
DOI: https://doi.org/10.7208/chicago/9780226570556.001.0001

Library of Congress Cataloging-in-Publication Data

Names: Smith, Bruce, 1946– author.
Title: Spill / Bruce Smith.
Other titles: Phoenix poets.
Description: Chicago ; London : The University of Chicago Press, 2018. |
    Series: Phoenix poets
Identifiers: LCCN 2017059452 | ISBN 9780226570419 (pbk. : alk. paper) |
    ISBN 9780226570556 (e-book)
Subjects: | LCGFT: Poetry.
Classification: LCC PS3569.M512 S67 2018 | DDC 811/.54—dc23
LC record available at https://lccn.loc.gov/2017059452

♾ This paper meets the requirements of ANSI/NISO Z39.48-1992
(Permanence of Paper).

For my brother Craig

Somewhere between the soul and soft machine

Is where I find myself again

MR. MISTER

So much rarc huge mystery taboo

Amiri Baraka

The Moments of Dominion
That happen on the Soul
And leave it with a Discontent
Too exquisite – to tell –

Emily Dickinson

We must endure our thoughts all night, until
The bright obvious stands motionless in cold.

Wallace Stevens

When my devotions could not pierce
        Thy silent eares;
Then was my heart broken, as was my verse

George Herbert

CONTENTS

Acknowledgments xi

Beautiful Throat *3*
Garden *4*
Summer Rain *5*
Raccoon *7*
Goodbye Tuscaloosa *9*
Ballad and Proposition *12*
Gaze *14*
What Are They Doing in the Next Room? *15*
The Whiteness *17*
Marvin Gaye Sings the National Anthem, 1983 *19*
"Are You Ready to Smash White Things?" *21*
Lewisburg *23*
Meat *43*
Run *45*
Boilermaker *47*
Bird *48*
Sister *50*
Button *51*
Pollen *53*
Honey *54*
True/False *56*
Ferment *57*
Index *59*

ACKNOWLEDGMENTS

The author gratefully acknowledges the editors of the publications where these poems first appeared:

Agni Online: "Once there was rage and the promise" as "Concussion Protocol"
American Poetry Review: "Button," "Honey," "Pollen," "True/False," "Goodbye Tuscaloosa"
Fogged Clarity: "Meat"
Jung Journal: Culture and Psyche: "Run," "Boilermaker, "'Are You Ready to Smash White Things?'"
Kenyon Review: "Ballad and Proposition," "Ferment," "Beautiful Throat," "Garden"
Los Angeles Review of Books: "Lewisburg" (as "1968")
Massachusetts Review: "Marvin Gaye Sings the National Anthem, 1983," "Summer Rain"
Ploughshares: "Raccoon"
Plume: "Bird," "The Whiteness" (as "White Project")
Poem-a-Day/Academy of American Poets: "What Are They Doing in the Next Room?"
Poetry Daily: "Garden"

To my beautiful, formidable, and fierce darlings, Jules and Megan.

To Bedros, Betsy and Greg and the Mandate of Heaven, Mike, Chard, Amy, Jeff, Claire, and Lane: my rabbis, my imams, my ministering angels.

To the American Academy in Rome and the Syracuse University Department of English.

To my mortified: Jack Wheatcroft, Denis Johnson, Pedro Cuperman.

Thanks to Martha Holland.

Once there was rage and the promise
that rage was a god not a corpse
message nor a melting of the core.
Once it moved us closer to weather
and thunder and it made poetry
as a cure. Then Herodotus broke
my heart with his history: his rumor
that begins as living twice and ends
as recompense for loss. Events bent me.
I took the arrow of accuracy in my eye.
The sugary accounts made me votary,
the biographical acids lashed my back.
I gave up songs for facts: those green
squawking parrots, that fire truck,
that earring, that body bound and gagged.
Then America broke my other heart
with its jails and gerrymandering,
its Emmett Till, its charms
and concussions, its ringing in my ears.
Who's the president? Who's your mother?
Who painted the angels? Who bombed
Homs? Repeat after me: comorbid,
torpid, transported. Close one eye. Hum.
Where's your mother's nation? Your father's
sky? Who's your other? Close the other eye.

Spill

BEAUTIFUL THROAT

Beheadings, slaughter of the innocents, suffering
and sorrow say all the stabbed, ecstatic art
of the museums and more of the same
says the news, the glowing, after glowing now
what, but also in the crowded galleries babies held
by mothers looking at babies being artfully held
in the celestial rain, the fat buttery ones, part putto,
part lard, who appear ready to slip from mother's arms
out of the frame into smoke and storm, the nonart part
of the world, that disobedient, expensive part
like a furious sea you paid to cross in an inflatable
plastic raft, a child's toy in a bath it looks like
from America where we have no fate
we can't make. Our stars are wire transfers
and firearms. Our future the bewitched mixture
of fuel with seawater with hubris that incinerates
the self. And character is the decree of childhood
evaporating into unauthorized space where the I/you
is so much questioning and answering nonart. In art
I see the gold leaf, the gashes, the beautiful throats
and hear the trauma arias of martyrdom
that are the same in nonart cities and deserts.
There are two schools: one that sings
the sheen and hues, the necessary pigments
and frankincense, while the world dries,
and the other voice like water that seeks
to saturate, erode, or spoil. It can't be handled.
It can't be marble. It wants to pool and vanish
and pour and soak the root systems. It ruins
as it changes as it saves.

GARDEN

I walked in the romantic garden and I walked
in the garden of ruin. I walked in the green-skinned,
black-skinned garden of Osiris who was ripped to pieces
and reformed and adored. I walked in that wet,
incestuous plot. Am I the only one who reads
for art? I walked in the garden of Amadou Diallo
whose shadow was punctured by unnumbered shafts
of light leading from West Africa to America where wallets
are guns. The chirp you heard in the garden as of two black
holes merging is what we call the soul. And when we cup
our hands to drink at the fountain we make the shape
of his skull. Am I the only one who reads for thirst?
I walked in the gardens of Houston where lizards
took their colors at the borders between terror and wonder,
dread and leafy glade, between silence and Sinatra.
I walked in Pope's garden in Twickenham that rhymed
wilderness and picturesque, walled in and out the stunted
self. In the garden of ruin new growth from the palms
I read as artful, neutral. In the romantic garden the fascists
sing, "I love you, I love you not." Statues in the gardens
are wrapped in Mylar blankets and blue plastic tarps
like refugees. I read them for reflection. I read for nation.
I read for color and form. In the orangery of Guantanamo,
in the grapevine of Babylon, I'm lost. I went there for the buzz,
the fiction of silence and a better self. Dressed sentimentally
in a dynamite suit in the garden of dates and pomegranates,
I read for patterns of the blast.

SUMMER RAIN

It's all butter and butter theft, thunder and the sloppy nature

of goodwill. It's all distress and excess, having it out

over home. The train station, the new cathedral.

The cathedral, the theater of murder, American-on-American

differences and distances, when some liquid machine starts

to slant the world, sets shadow in motion, a sky-

blue tarp the new heaven, rain on skin the new numen,

pepper spray at the borders the new sentiment,

the new outcast fate. Two shoes ruined, chewed by shepherds

of the devil, the vamp and tongue demolished like

what Nina Simone did to a song, cleaving it

to/from home. How long before the outsole

is ripped from the pink insole and the shank,

a leathery flag of your surrender

to all the parts of speech that fail

    to represent objects, subjects, qualities, or states?

Air swarms to a certain density that appears

    as *one you hurried to when you were troubled,*

Dickinson said her mother wasn't.

    And of her father, *the oldest and oddest sort*

of foreigner. A sweater and water, the new

    father and mother, Republican and ghost, a far-fetched

thing replaced with law or storm or idle kindness from afar.

RACCOON

A man with CRCK on his snapback. A man in a BLDBTH hoodie
[what happened to the affable vowels?]. I stay shy of the men
on the bus because we know who we are. We are propelled
by kimchee and cologne that smells of diesel fuel and demon.
Five hours of trance and hard consonants. I find a seat
next to Grace Paley, lit by a tiny beam, who asks, Is there room
for the unredeemed? She offers me a hard candy, says,
Do the dead ride for free? And then we do what the dead,
discounted do, we open a thin, neat bound book and read
as if that would feed or suffer or cut someone with its white
pages. Heat and the damp flames of us subtract the oxygen
from the air that boredom sharpened into despair.
This is the time between the shy, nocturnal creatures
with dilated eyes and the diminished ones that ransack the burnt-
over places. At Big Daddy's we stop to pick up the escapees
from the second and third great awakenings. These visionaries
have seen the ruby of the brake lights and have gone forward
to be shattered and to be known by Grace. They have bundled
and touched one another in a marriage sanctioned by the vowels
of the Onondaga Nation. Could each of us have, please,
a more modest incline and a moon we could douse like a raccoon
douses the world? Its name means *brother who scrubs*
everything. Grace says, The story is not the cargo. The story
is a couple of hours and a cold sandwich you eat and it vanishes
into you in the lights of the oncoming and in the fundamentalist war
between moving and keeping still. It [bus, breath, voice, distance]
is a longhouse that smells like a city of roasting meats, smothered fires,
sewage, and perfumes, where hate and pleasure can live, almost cordially
if we relinquish our convictions. The invention of need in a lost language

happened here with a word or two doused in the dark. A woman
with a piece of toast who shivers. A woman with opera-mask slippers.
And then a word that fails as soon as it is spoken, an exhaustion
that's a form of pleasure, although Grace says, Whose pleasure? Whose work?

GOODBYE TUSCALOOSA

Goodbye Rufus and Ditzy, Goodbye Don Dove, Goodbye Tim Early,
    Goodbye Bebe Barefoot.
Goodbye to the Brooklyn Jewboos and the boys from Des Moines
    who wandered in their trail of tears to Tuscaloosa.
Goodbye to the Ur ovens of Woodrow's. I loved the slaughtered hog,
    the gloried grease, the human nature standing around the fire.
Goodbye to the state flower—the shredded layer of rubber
    the truckers call alligators.
Goodbye to my face in the window at night.
Goodbye to the songs I sang to you beginning in bright vocals
    continuing to the dark lies and ending
    in parlando where our burdens are put down.
Goodbye to those I could not understand and could not understand me.
    When you said, "Troy," I heard, "Charlie."
Goodbye All-American Storage and my birthright exchanged for a mess of postage.
Goodbye rained-on cardboard box. Goodbye corrugation—chart of my heart.
    Goodbye roach, you were my ontology.
Goodbye wind twisted in the Gulf and slapped
    and spun through Tupelo
    and sent like the *po*-lice to the homes of the poor.
Goodbye Druid City Car Wash whose spray was scrupulous to me at two ayem,
    whose mist was an exercise by Saint Ignatius
    on sympathy with the suffering.
Goodbye to my face in the window at night.
Goodbye Blondel. Goodbye Aquanetta.
Goodbye, too, to the West Alabama Veterinary Clinic where I waited
    with the sick furred thing with the owners of Wabbles,
    L'l G'l, Dollbaby, Mrs. Pinkerton, and Honey Bun
    for yours is the pure devotion.

Goodbye to the Crimson Tide fans who worshipped the hypermasculine
    for yours is the pure devotion.
Goodbye Mr. Vaughn of the 103rd bomber squadron, blind, kind, for no
      white reason.
Goodbye to the machinery of the horizon and the fried foods of Ezell's
    Catfish Shack,
    where I could taste my mud and slumber.
Goodbye crepe myrtle and the vertigo of the last hundred years.
    When I lived here [there] George Wallace died,
    the coach was fired, and you were my alibi.
Goodbye three hours' drive to M'fs. Goodbye elsewhere.
Goodbye red Camaro in a black bra. Goodbye hairdo as the Kabuki
    of the South. Goodbye blues.
    If there's a labial among y'all, let it be heard now.
Goodbye Alfonso. Goodbye Tyrone. Goodbye Stella. Goodbye student
    who prayed for me in my sin and affliction.
Goodbye freight train for yours was the pure devotion.
Goodbye nights of the fragrance I never named and days of noon, tongue,
    and handgun.
Goodbye manners as tongue and handgun.
Goodbye unknown woman with a drink in her hand who burst through the
      tea olive,
    without spilling, walking in the back and out the front door.
    I kiss your Jack and Coke goodbye.
Goodbye to the bird saying "Preacher, Preacher."
Goodbye to the dirty silence clarified. Here's my reparation.
    Here's my face in the window at night.
Goodbye to the 4x4s on lawns and the Pain Care Center.
    I became an orphan like you here [there].
    There was no shade for me under pin oak or magnolia.
Goodbye to the Black Orchid and your transvestites. Goodbye Miss
    Mystery.
    I kiss your post-op lips goodbye.
Goodbye and thanks for the Jesus.

Goodbye Time as a pure form of sensuous intuition. Goodbye Immanuel Kant
    of Queen City Boulevard.
Goodbye Bible verse on the cash-register receipt.
Goodbye pool hall, cabstand, pawnshop, and storm-door company.
Goodbye "He's as rude as a Yankee."
Goodbye red velvet cake and ersatz rue.
Goodbye Little Zion Tabernacle Church with your brush arbor
    built from wood milled in the hollow
    and your darker than blue.
Goodbye bathtub covered with a mattress during the tornado.
    You took my form.
Goodbye tetchy, goodbye triflin', goodbye mama love and moon pie.
Goodbye my little scuppernong.
Goodbye interlocutor with the lost. I kiss you reluctantly
    as one kisses the forehead of the child
    whose fever will kill.
Goodbye to the Enola Gay of race, and to Mr. Vaughn, who flew in you,
    blind, kind for no white reason.
    Thank you for the two-dollar bill.
Let me lie down between Rama Lama's and Vinyl Solutions one last time.
Let me lie down between the porch and the battle reenactment,
    the bombers and the lambs,
    the bonfires and the birthplace of Sun Ra.

Wisteria crushing the tin shed cannot find me.
From now on the law against kudzu is lifted.
From now on I will be translated into this.
You were my Dollywood. I was your Judas.
    Maybe some Tara will save me.
I will look back.
I will become cold and salted.
I will go up into the morning, sometimes.
I will be measured. I will be shattered.

BALLAD AND PROPOSITION

after Alice Oswald

Take away my engine and I shall engineless go
to find you. Take away my bees
and I will flowerless walk the vectors of sweet
nothings until I'm face-to-face with Monsanto.

In my doomed town where small mechanic skills
make the evenings strung out and shrill
with compressors and vapors, I listen for crows
and wrens to overdub our nation's ills,

which are forgetting and further forgetting
so I don't recognize my hand,
the length of rope, the knot, the limb
I throw it over, the aid and abetting

of the body. The shadow spans from Senegal
to my doomed town where Mrs. White
cuts off a limb that drops its intractable
leaves in menacing random and illegal

patterns on her lawn. The proposition
is to each cut off a limb, a sacrifice to prevent
destructions more terrible in the future,
as did the Sioux. Because I lack imagination

somebody, a Christ, a boy in custody, dies
each evening. Three days' wait and I forget
the undertaking, the uprising, that way
of life with redemption. I forget the lies

modified by art. I forget the ongoing
story of love tending toward catastrophe,
the oblique, gaped, murderous corridos
ending in the underworld and unknowing.

GAZE

My guide and I first purified before the sacrifice,
but can you be purified, I asked her, without being banished
or erased? My guide said, it's always *but* with you, why
can't you just archive the whiteness or curate the liquidity
of the city and play your music or whatever you do? Here,
she said, is where the runaway slaves made a way through,
a cut through the thicket, a hairline crack in the salty progress
and the saccharine business of April, there, can you see it?
I don't see it, I can't see it, I said, I see mud and the under/
over story and gold-green buds like a child's coloring.
What were their names? Names? she said. They had spoilage
like fruit and a market price and an exchange rate but no names.
The shining things of your city are their names. But
what did they call each other when they rhymed, I said,
when they licked the salt off one another? It's always rhyme
with you, she said. They called each other what lovers
call each other after they've been worked from can't see to
can't see: orphan and mi alma and baby and flaca and boo.
It's always history with you, I said. It's always ecstasy with you,
she said. We walked. It was trash day, translucent bags
in front of the church, pearlescent swelling cases like frog spawn.
Black bags in front of the shelter, little todesfugues,
minimal deskilled art. The cans are brutes or toters,
makeshift mausoleums or stops along the sublime,
equal in size to the body if it were smashed and bound,
leaking out pork-chop bones, silvers, oils. Rats and crows
rip into human resource and order. Look at the relics
from Byzantium. Look at the maggots and the rubies.

WHAT ARE THEY DOING IN THE NEXT ROOM?

Are they unmaking everything?
Are they tuning the world sitar?
Are they taking an ice pick to Being?
Are they enduring freedom in Kandahar?

Sounds, at this distance, like field hollers,
sounds like they'll be needing CPR.
Sounds like the old complaint of love and dollars.
Sounds like when Coltrane met Ravi Shankar

and the raga met the rag and hearing
became different and you needed CPR
after listening and tearing was tearing
and love was a binary star—

distant bodies eclipsing each other
with versions of gravity and light.
Sounds like someone's trying to smother
the other—a homicide or a wedding night.

The television derives the half-full hours.
Time exists as mostly what's to come.
Losing also is ours . . .
I meant that as a question.

Is *I* the insomniac's question?
Are *you* a dendrite or a dream?
Between oblivion and affection,
which one is fear and which protection?

Are they transitive or in?
Are they process or product?
Are they peeling off the skin?
Are they Paris or the abducted?

They're reading something after Joyce,
postmodern stuff that can be read
but not understood except as voices
rising and falling from the dead.

Do they invent me
as I invent their faces?
I see surveillance gray wasted
with bliss at having thieved identities.

In the a.m., when *tú* turns to *usted*,
the sun clocks in to overwrite the night
with hues and saturations and the red
hesitates, for a second, to be incarnate.

THE WHITENESS

The dream was clean of all indebtedness.
I owed nobody nothing. I was in my skin
although there was a voice in the distance,
bees, maybe, or a fire or an ocean. I woke
in the white project, white noise in the ongoing
occupation. I woke in the future perfect tense
where I will have been immediately released
from the reckoning of my dream after serving
the mandatory minimum. I will have been
immediately treated for my pain. I will have
added years to my life, bank to my bank, unbent
some notes, attended, heard: words were spoken
to me and I comprehended. I heard. I was
lavishly defended. I was less arrested, more
gently delayed. Wires worked for me,
transmitting, distributing the currency, our way
of life. Clouds worked for me, optics,
lawyers, nature, flattery: the hands of the praying
mantis, the eye of the hurricane, gravity.
The weight at the end of the rope
worked for me, the statute, the plastic
explosive, the xylem and phloem in a tree.
Worked for me. Was that singing sung for me?
I played the lottery and lost, but the silver
I scratched off fell like vulcanized spectral
snow. Losing was a luxury I could afford.
Still I had the itch from the scratch
tickets and called it character. I called it
ambition. I called it milk and penicillin,

called it complexion. Angels explained.
I heard and I abided with a slight fatigue.
I felt flushed. I felt fundamentally pale.
In my mind were the spirals and stars
for which I was treated with the world.

MARVIN GAYE SINGS THE NATIONAL ANTHEM, 1983

at the NBA All-Star game and nothing changes
for Marvin or the nation, yet everything changes

in the 2 minutes and 35 seconds of voice and drum
machine as he sings "stars" in 5 syllables as if counting

the points of a stylized luminous thing. He sings
as if he were the nomenclator for a dim-witted king

running ahead of the slow procession and running
back with the names of Moses, Magic, Dr. J/

Julius Erving, Bird, and No. 33, Kareem Abdul-Jabbar,
whose name means Noble One, Servant of the Almighty.

Augur of energy and culture and almost unbearable
presence, he sings at the shadow play of hurt and healing,

in the theater of race and sex, mercy and money
where absurdly vertical male figures are standing

at a certain angle to violence and women and the world
executing the killer crossover, sneakers squealing

from child labor. It's basketball, Jack. It's art under halogen
lights with hate and humorlessness removed. Marvin sings

"ramparts" with sincerity and irony as if he were keeping
watch on the battlements for Hamlet's father's ghost.

Who's there? he asks in a double-breasted suit
and mirrored shades and pocket silk. He removes

one stone from apartheid. He sings and it's treason.
It's Reagan. It's strategic marketing. It's miscegenation.

It's cocaine chopped and snorted off a mirror reflecting
the dilated decade. He takes the British drinking

song of bonhomie and puts it through a war and the forgetting.
He sings so far behind the beat it's as if he's remembering

the beatings, the burden, the chitlin' circuit, asking
is it more or less beautiful now and was it the singing?

"ARE YOU READY TO SMASH WHITE THINGS?"

Nina Simone said in Harlem, 1969, but failed to incite a riot.
Music for all its pluck, for all its rubs and inflamed
moments in the feet and hands, its palaces of breath and math,
for all the buzz and wail that day, was an affirmative fail.
It does not mean that music fails or it fails to be music
or that there are not vibrations from the radical core
or the sound of bees from the boundary layers or bursts
from sheer instabilities that pick up speed and leave
acoustic signatures and infrasounds that can be delivered
years later as dust and tears in Missouri or Anadarko,
Oklahoma, where we hid from the supercells of funnel clouds
[which are white or dark depending on power flashes] under
the lintels and gripped the jambs while the landspout shadowed us
then removed everything that was a house. Around us trash.
So smash the laws of large numbers and thermodynamics,
smash low pressure and incomprehensible flow. Smash
angular, black-and-white Kansas with its cruel neighbors.
Smash Oz and my house there and my father's house
where there are many luminous mansions. Smash mansions
and Professor Marvel. Smash the easy, the expedient,
the confidence man. Smash the estate. Smash the hoax.
Smash home and the subprime. Smash the man
behind the curtain. Smash the curtain. Smash the exposition
and the rising action, the southern strategy and what passes
for compassion. Smash the passes. Smash the deep sleep
of the '80s, the influenza of star wars. Smash private equity.
Smash the glass darkly. Smash the fluffy white cloud. Smash
the debt and the tenuous grip on the tender. Smash the knowing.

Smash 3/5 of anything. Smash the quid pro quo. Smash
the composure. Smash walking down the obedient street
listening to the new without hearing the old cluster of notes,
the pressures in the air, the violently coiled cloud.

LEWISBURG

By June, by muggy, iffy June of 1968 I had received a draft notice [1-A, report to Fort Dix], a degree in English [undistinguished], and six [or more] concussions from playing college football. I was waiting to be seized by the roots of my hair from the roofs of Philadelphia, where I was working mopping hot tar, and dropped into the jungle, Canada, or jail.

Instead, that July I started work as a teacher at the federal penitentiary in Lewisburg, Pennsylvania.

Work: a chance to find yourself, as Conrad said in *Heart of Darkness*. But by 1968 Conrad and work were already discredited. Look at our fathers in their ironed shirts. Look at our steaming mothers.

I believed in the thaumaturgical, the wonder work like the kind that snatched my father back from the fiery wreck of WWII and dropped him into an elementary school as a teacher. Seedlings in cups, cutout snowflakes, a rabbit, naps. That summer in Philadelphia I looked into the bubbling cauldron of black pitch in the "Hotmaster" kettle and saw the hell realm black as James Brown's hair, black as a rice paddy at night. I went to work like a stickup man, in a hat, sunglasses, long sleeves, and a bandana over my face, but still, like Lou Reed sang in "Coney Island Baby," a kid *playing football for the coach*. My tar mop was an extension of my mother's mop, my father's mop swabbing the decks. In the chimerical heat like jet exhaust shimmering from the roofs I had visions: I would be rescued or translated into vapors or made dead by the voodoo of the age.

The age: Malcolm El-Shabazz dead, MLK, *the drum major for peace, for righteousness*, dead, RFK dead, fire in the cities, sex, Tet, destroying the town in order to save it, body bags on the runways, one hit then quit shit, *mutual pleasure mutual power* the marching women said, music painting a thin black lacquer over everything, Otis Redding dead, the great god Brown screaming *Please*, Aretha demanding "Respect," OM vibrating in Coltrane's skull, Philadelphia's own Delfonics delivering their blows by falsetto.

Students for a Democratic Society [SDS] seemed like a natural extension of my reading of the Romantic poets [Shelley: "the devotion to something afar/from the sphere of our sorrow"] and rage against the war and the affliction of capital. I joined. It seemed like what you did when you took off your helmet for the last time. Plus they needed a center fielder for the softball team.

My first week at the penitentiary I took a blow to the back of my head and was kicked in the ribs by one tense individual who didn't make parole. I had witnessed his hearing as part of my [dis]orientation. I let go of the notion of the innocent criminal, although I held onto the notion of my own innocence. I resisted the romance of the prison, which was another kind of romance. Disoriented: I lost my East. I lost my West too.

The guards must have looked at me and thought *buffoon*, a young punk pretending to be a radical priest, and so, *fuck him on general principles.* To the inmates, to whom style in its condition of deprivation—the rolled cuff, the Converse high-tops, the collar—was everything, a survival tool, sympathetic magic, and a costume, I must have looked like someone fallen from the Platonic ideal of style into the exigencies of Shirt City. I was compliant and defiant in my costume. I wore my sport coat and tie to satisfy the warden's edict. I died a little and was reborn in a houndstooth coat and a pocket silk. But I strutted like an NBA point guard and paraded about in the late '60s paisley or magenta shirt/tie ensemble. The response from inmates included some pity for the hot mess that I was and some "slip me some skin" [no other contact was permitted]. The guards squinted and said, "Go ahead."

Processed, "re-educated through labor" [Mao Zedong], intimidated, I
signed a release, signed away my life in case I was held hostage [although
the language was much more convoluted]. With other intakes I was
photographed in a photo booth, like at a boardwalk amusement park—
half banquette, half curtain, three beeps, four flashes. Instead of my
terrified, thick-necked white face, a strip of four black faces dropped in
the slot. Two profiles, two toothy smiles, subtitled with numbers of the
last guy—*mon semblable, mon frère!* My first identity disorder. My first
fiction.

Years go by. I mean that as a question. Storage of memory is not retrieval of
memory—retrieval is part will and part unwilling neural tide. Memory
of ratting my way through the corridors comes back, unbidden, like a
particular smell—only a fraction of a fraction of a microparticle will set
off an olfactory memory, and then I am revisiting a taste of blood from
a human sacrifice at Ur. Retrieval is a time snatch, requires a deft athletic
maneuver or a stumbling fall, or some of both.

It is like retrying a case, bringing the experience back into a courtroom full
of sensationalizing reporters and grieving spectators, family members,
ex-lovers. Everybody has a stake in the outcome. Everyone has a version
of what happened and an opinion and a plea. Most of them wrong
about everything. There are prosecutors and defendants, a judge and a
jury selected from your high-school teachers all loud in your head and
struggling to be heard. And the entire proceedings are conducted using
lines of poems from Emily Dickinson. *My Life had stood—a Loaded Gun.*
Or *Before I got my eye put out.*

Was I hired at the jail because I was the young collegiate altruist with some
Spanish? No, I was there because I ran recklessly and with abandon as a
halfback [Coach Huntress, I am your boy] and collided with other thick-
necked individuals and so they thought, those administrators in Prison
Education, that I could protect myself.

To get there I drove William Penn Drive, or Pen Drive, in the nomenclature of the joint. Heartbreak Ridge Road slanted off to the left. It led the back way to Big House Circle and Dairy Barn Road as if this were a parody of a suburban development. My route was down a road visible in its entirety from the tower. Guards and inmates alike could see me coming a mile away in my convertible as I performed free, white, and twenty-one.

I walked through seven hot electric locks from the fake Florentine tower where guards surveyed everything to my place in Education. "When I hear the word culture . . . I release the safety on my Browning!" says a character in the play *Schlageter*, by Nazi poet laureate Hanns Johst. Enter, stage left, me, as uneasy emissary of Culture.

Class, race, and gender as I knew them in their safe ratios were shattered in the cauldron of the joint. [Shattered too was Light, Space, Time.] Class: under, mixed with radical other. Race: 70 percent Black and Hispanic. Gender: all male cast, violently heterosexual, violently homosexual. A vocal brown majority replaced Nixon's silent white majority. Inmates looked at the warden's picture of the president on top of the business deployment flowchart with amused hatred. Class was broken down into the dream of American classlessness [everyone wearing the same Navy fatigues] and then reorganized into gangs of color, power, and gender not unlike the culture at large. Things got unzipped. Overturned, tore up, or stood on their heads.

Or stood facing the wall with an instrument, as if by some Orphic power of lung and reed and fingering the wall would fall down. The myth was if you got good enough with your horn, the wall would crumble and you would walk out into the promised land. In the same vein: the mock presidential election held inside for those who couldn't vote yielded Alabama Governor George Wallace as the winner. Why? I asked an inmate. "Wallace win and the wall come down." The place had its grandiloquent ways.

The prison was lit like an operating room, like a train station, the back of
a high-school physics classroom, a monastery, the barracks at Fort Dix.
How could it be dim and dazzling at the same time? I had no Foucault to
describe the light. "Of course you know the work of Frantz Fanon?" my
teacher's aide said. Had I known Fanon I would have been able to speak
of the blackness: *a drop of sun under the earth.*

My teacher's aide, S, an inmate, spoke three languages and studied with
Timothy Leary and Richard Alpert [now Baba Ram Dass] at Harvard in
the League for Spiritual Discovery. S's advanced degree in psychology was
trumped by an honorary doctorate in insouciance he earned in jail. He got
busted in Texas crossing the border in his Volkswagen Beetle, a first offense
for possession of pot [which sounds like the synopsis of a Janis Joplin
song]. I imagined him being held upside down on a pole. "Bring that boy
on in here," he said the judge said. A light-skinned African-American from
Boston; S became my mentor, my jazz rabbi, my alma mater.

S stole books for me from the prison library and stamped the edges with
"Property of the Catholic Chaplain" so when my person and possessions
were inspected by the guards on my way out I was guaranteed a safe
passage.

The Tibetan Book of the Dead; *Notes from the Underground*; Kafka; Wilde;
The Wretched of the Earth and *Black Skin, White Masks* by Fanon; Alan
Watts; *The Electric Kool-Aid Acid Test*; McLuhan; *Black Elk Speaks*; *The
Portable Nietzsche*, publishers' overstocks sent to the federal penitentiary
as humanitarian [tax-deductible] gifts to reform the incarcerated. No
poems. Books by men, yes, but not "manly man" books. Books by men
destabilized by time, as was I.

I was wrong about everything, the Muslims told me, and I salaamed.

The Aryans wanted signs of solidarity. They offered unconditional hatred for everybody else. The protection they offered was, they said, "bumper to bumper."

War resisters, drug lords, drug mules, addicts, atomic spies, counterfeiters, bootleggers, pimps, distillers of moonshine, killers of your mother, your sister, your brother, white power brokers, black panthers, white-collar administrators doing what they were told, hammers and the nailed, extorters, innocents, crossers of state lines, tax evaders, peckerwoods, jury tamperers: what did I know, really, about who they were? Who was I? I was wrong about everything. I was too shy to ask about the crime, the time, "the bid." No one told me about snapping someone's neck. No one told me about the stabbing. In class we solved math problems about time and space and corrected mistakes in grammar. "Whose grammar?" the Muslims asked.

"Hey, Mr. SDS, come over here a minute. See this? This is what they can do with a pen. If you've got enough time anything can be sharpened. This is what we found in a cell. One cell. So you can multiply this by ten or a hundred and ten. Can you multiply? Homemade piece of mayhem with a purpose. Or maybe someone smuggled something in in someone's rectum. This here could go into your heart up to here between your ribs. Look at the rest of this stuff we shook down. Don't get too close, SDS. Don't get too smoochy."

I ate lunch at the officers' mess, not with the general population. I ate well through the largesse of the underground economy. I was fed desserts denied to the officers: blueberry cobblers, some peach thing, snickerdoodles, strudel, crisps. An Aryan left a pudding on my table. The inmates waited on me like indulgent grandmothers. The phrase *stick it to the man* was in current usage. Was I not the man?

Premise: All inmates get an eighth-grade education. Premise: To get paroled inmates need a job, which means a twelfth-grade education. Therefore: I get a job teaching GED classes to bridge the gap. The best students devoted themselves in a way I have not seen since; a year's work of high-school math would be completed in a week. The worst slept facedown on the desk, inert, wronged, drooling, unable to be roused, with darkness behind the eyes, *in the blue room* of their depression like their collegiate others.

The dance of my freedom went like this: jail, not-jail—a two-step that included evenings at the bar, Dunkle's [German for dark]. In not-jail I squirmed under the hot blanket of my draft notice, dreaming of a hand clamped on my shoulder that would escort me to a jeep that drove me to the head of the Ho Chi Minh trail. I read the stolen books and Baraka, Lao Tzu, the Gita, the Koran. I dropped thirty pounds in not-jail. I was the metaphor, the aperture into our symptoms, carrying across the news of the extremity and pornography, the thin membrane between the forbidden and the permitted. I spun tales as foamy and insipid as the beer, stories in which I was the hero who survived another day of mayhem in this fucked-up world. Fucked-up: it elected Nixon and put the Berrigans behind bars. A woman I met was writing a thesis on conspiracy theories and the Kennedy assassination.

Cigarettes were currency. Dental floss, a photograph, a sock. A tin of mackerel, a palm frond, pills. A taste of an envelope someone had laced with acid could be traded on the commodities market like Sumerians trading coins and barley. Anything in foil. Anything sharp. A lipstick, a lick of something, cum. I brought in a roll of tropical fruit Life Savers— fruit punch, piña colada, tangerine, banana, and mango melon—and gave them to S who told me they could buy almost a life and did I have more?

I read about Saint Genet, but I had no Antonio Gramsci and his letters from
   prison to help me read the cultural dominion. No Dietrich Bonhoeffer
   to offer me a Christian resistance. No Eldridge Cleaver, *Soul on Ice*
   [confiscated at the gate with my pen]. No James Baldwin, *Fire Next Time*.
   Really? James Baldwin? I was wrong about everything, the guards told
   me. "The degree of civilization in a society can be judged by entering
   its prisons," Dostoyevsky said. *Come back again to the jail, Oscar Wilde,*
   honey.

I had no poetry in my life. I had read some poetry in college, but it had not
   yet entered my heart or been stuck between my ribs.

Buffalo Township, Union County, where the guards and caseworkers lived,
   voted overwhelmingly for Barry Goldwater in 1964. "In Your Heart You
   Know He's Right," the billboard said. "Yeah, far right," my leaning-left
   mother said, echoing the joke.

"Of course you're familiar with the work of Miles Davis," S said. He said to
   go get *Sketches of Spain* and *E.S.P.* "Or are you listening to Streisand?"
   I tried to buy vinyl at the Woolworth's in Lewisburg where they did sell
   Streisand but no Miles. I felt the accretion of my ignorance as a form of
   whiteness. And I felt my whiteness as a terminal sentence. I wanted to
   hear Miles. I felt insulted [by whom I didn't know] but sharpened enough
   by my jail time to slash my way, with a mind-forged knife, through the
   pitiful accumulation of American commodities and oil excrescences and
   non-prison capital and storefronts with no Miles and Barry Goldwater
   and the Pennsylvania Dutch cuisine and the buttery white light and rows
   of corn until I got to Big House Circle via Heartbreak Ridge Road and
   from the outside blew my horn against the wall.

"Hey, SDS, is that a matching shirt, tie, and pocket square? I have my eye on
   you, meat."

30

I was asked to direct a play, *12 Angry Men*, a TV drama that was made into a film in 1957 about a homicide trial in which eleven of twelve men are wrong about everything. Unlike the original, I had a cast of seven black actors to work with. "How can you be positive about anything?" Lee J. Cobb asks in the movie. When that line was delivered by a brother in the prison production, it brought down the house. [And still the walls were unmoved.]

Fridays in Education there was sometimes a film, although the administration didn't like the idea of darkening down a room. Most were stultifying advertisements, made for white America, about timber and the telephone. One was from the National Film Board of Canada, Oscar Peterson playing piano over a slow pan of women on beaches in the Maritime Provinces, and we held ourselves for an hour and thought of Canada and the female form.

Muhammad Speaks, The Village Voice, The Berkeley Barb, The Evergreen Review were in circulation in the prison. And I couldn't bring in James Baldwin?

I distributed the programmed GED books in language arts and math. Could I multiply? Eleven times eleven equals what? Nice pentameter S said. This is how the hours went in Education. I tried to explain the subjective and objective cases: Let's *you and I* or *you and me* go to the concert? The books still reeked of postwar GI workforce sweat and illustrated math problems with towheaded kids in sweaters gathering apples in bushels. I devised my own problems: *If three gallons of gasoline can burn four city blocks. . . .* S taught me how to consult the oracle of the *I Ching*. "Let's give the *Ching* a ring," he said. We used the Bolligen edition translated by Wilhelm and Baynes, with an introduction by Carl Jung. In place of ancient coins or yarrow stalks we ripped up paper and tossed them heads, tails to divine our future. S read the hexagram: Straight line, straight line, straight line, broken line, straight line, straight line:

Hsiao Ch'u—The Taming Power of the Small

If you are sincere, blood vanishes and fear gives way.
No blame.

I witnessed the death of an inmate after he drank most of a tin of duplicating
fluid meant for the mimeograph machine. He thrashed like a mackerel
on the floor of Education. Whatever prison status I earned by taking a
beating, I lost when I fainted.

"Prison" as an adjective meant parochial, narrow, concocted with inadequate
resource, with limited vision and effect. Prison tattoos, prison liquor.
It meant broke-dick, jury-rigged, ghetto. Prison lawyers, prison air-
conditioning, prison logic. Prison light, prison space, prison time.
Insufficient in knowledge and power and yet admirable, a nonstyle that
earns begrudging, righteous respect for its style. I was a prison teacher.

"Get poor," Father Philip Berrigan said. He arrived at Lewisburg at the end
of the year. I never met him although he too taught in Education before
he transferred to the minimum-security facility at Allenwood. "In such
a war," he said about Vietnam, though he could have meant prison, too,
"man stands outside the blessings of God."

It was a place of overwhelming materiality. [It was a fucking rock.] A
1932 *Popular Science* article about the new Lewisburg prison under
construction illustrates the obvious: the masonry of "block and bar"
walls and the "carbon steel bars with tool-proof steel cases." Against the

weight of the corporal came an opposing push from the metaphysical, not just from the Office of the Catholic Chaplain or the Nation of Islam. ["The material/spiritualizes and lock stone and air meet/cordially with a high lust clamping one to the other," A. R. Ammons says in *Garbage*. "Finite to fail, but infinite to venture," says Emily Dickinson]. The real got tested every day by its opposite. The obvious and opaque became porous. There is vacuity in things, as Lucretius said, even stone, concrete, carbon steel. Hurt was a lever to pry open the cover to the real. Skin, too, was a microthickness that could be cut, it was a sign of your tribe, your fleshy sentence, and, when pressed, your ticket to ride. A pigeon flying by the window, a cloud, a cuff, a sigh could be the vehicle for the transcendental. Things scarred over or got subtle. It was possible for everyone to be a bodhisattva. Or at least a surrealist or a fetishist.

Baba Ram Dass handled S's parole. He wrote from India to say, "The bars are in your mind."

"We who live in prison, and in whose lives there is no event but sorrow, have to measure time by throbs of pain, and the record of bitter moments."
—Oscar Wilde

"I talked to 'em," Richard Pryor said when he spent six weeks on location at the Arizona State Penitentiary making the 1980 film *Stir Crazy*, "and thank God we got penitentiaries."

There's no such thing as silence composer John Cage called his 1952 work. And in the jail the same: a duration with coughs, screams, snores, the percussion, and amplified metal on metal. The stamp, pat, thigh-slap, clap of someone doing his hambone. Nocturne for things sharpened over time.

I was wrong about the categories, the binaries, S told me. I was wrong about who was weak and who was strong, ruthless and kind, gay and straight.

Prison radio had three modes: country, jazz, and rhythm and blues. All dedicated in their way to bringing the wall down. A point of honor to be true to your school. Prison honor. No crossovers. No defectors.

Inmates in my class insisted, then posted, then consulted daily, like they would results at OTB, what they called the Hall of Shame/Hall of Fame, a lined sheet of paper as in grade school to which they added, justly or unjustly, the names of their friends and enemies.

"I do not doubt interiors have their interiors, and exteriors have their exteriors—and that the eye-sight has another eye-sight, and the hearing another hearing, and the voice another voice"—Walt Whitman, "Assurances"

I was ordered [you could do that in jail] to discontinue the Hall of Shame/ Hall of Fame by the head of Education, a small groundhog of a man who seemed to have dug under a posthole in the New Hampshire woods and then surfaced inside the wall in Pennsylvania. Too much agitation, he said, which meant there was taunting and retaliation and a beatdown over the rankings and someone was spending some time in the hole.

The prison shrink befriended me, asked if I'd be willing to sit in with his group, a therapy group, or T-group, where inmates were encouraged to express their feelings. I told S there was only one feeling, which was expressed each week: somebody on his knees pounding on the chair with his fists.

Sung—Conflict

The Judgment

Conflict. You are sincere
And are being obstructed.
A cautious halt halfway brings good fortune.
Going through to the end brings misfortune.
It furthers one to see the great man.
It does not further one to cross the great water.

My mother, my beautiful mother, the ex-marine, called me to say, "Sit down. Are you sitting down?" I sat to hear I was to report for my Army physical. I packed for Canada. I ran down the hallway of my apartment in the hope I could throw myself against the wall and induce a final, army-disqualifying injury. Another concussion, a separation. I reported for my exam with my X-rays from football and letters from doctors to prove I had had at least six traumatic brain injuries. "You're a specimen, son. You passed. Tell your mother the good news."

On the stairs to Education someone said, "Blood the fuck up."

On the stairs to Education some scuffling or buttoning up or down [were zippers permitted?] some cloth rustling. I saw a black hand, supine, brush fingertips with a white hand, prone, passing some powder maybe or a Life Saver or just a forbidden touch.

S told me he spent the weekend licking some stamps that had been franked, read by his caseworker, and passed on to him. The stamps were steeped in acid.

At the end of August I would watch on television the four nights of coverage of the Democratic National Convention in Chicago. [On a borrowed black-and-white Westinghouse portable with a "See-Matic" chassis and a wide range four-inch speaker.] I knew that the general population could only watch television up to nine o'clock, so it was up to me to report what I witnessed the next day: I saw Mayor Daley swearing at Senator Abe Ribicoff of Connecticut. [I couldn't hear him say, "Fuck you, you Jew son of a bitch."] I saw tear gas and schools of anti-war protestors like fish in underwater shades of gray in Grant Park. [I couldn't see the Yippie Festival of Life or the police riot of the *Walker Report*.] I saw turmoil on the floor of the convention. [I couldn't see Dan Rather getting punched in the stomach.] I saw kids my age being clubbed and Maced and arrested and bandaged. I saw cops in helmets swinging their nightsticks. I saw tanks and the National Guard like in Philadelphia. [I wouldn't hear until later, "The whole world is watching."] I could see the rough beast. [I couldn't see Bethlehem]. I could see there was one feeling being expressed and a reaction to that feeling by the police. But I was seized. I tried to convey to S and others in Education what it was, what it was like. *It was some fucked up shit, man* was the best I could do. It was the "flabby, pretending, weak-eyed devil of a rapacious and pitiless folly." But S told me *Heart of Darkness* was racist, man.

But I was a witness. For the first time I was needed for my testimony. S and some other political prisoners [We're all political prisoners, S said] would wait for me inside the classroom of Education. Prison waiting: "sweating the fence." It was a ritual that was both urgent and indifferent, a jolted boredom, a slouching, enervated attention, for the news I could barely carry. "Spill," S said, and I spilled my crude account. I made a vow to get articulate, like Malcolm X. Or if not articulate I could aspire toward a "curious puffing . . . whispering heavenly labials in a world of gutturals," as Wallace Stevens says, in order to undo the powers that be.

T'ung Jên—Fellowship with Men

Nine in the fifth place means:
Men bound in fellowship first weep and lament,
But afterward they laugh.
After great struggles they succeed in meeting.

Vietnam was my demon. Part exotic nature show, part Hollywood blowin'
stuff up, part crime drama, part elegy. It was a naked girl running from
her napalmed village. It was a black-and-white shadow show that depicted
the signal grasses being bent severely down by the rotors of a helicopter
while young men my age were carrying stretchers with fubared young
men my age. I watched it every night. It was my destination. Vietnam was
my military other that followed me, leaning over me at night looking for a
vein to start an IV drip.

My mother called. "Are you sitting down? You got a letter. I opened it.
You've got a date to report to Fort Dix."

I put in eight-hour days, but sometimes I would leave to eat and come
back for a T-group or play practice. I did my time. My friend, the prison
shrink, invited me to join his NA [Narcotic Anonymous] group. *We need
somebody who is neither an inmate nor a guard, a sort of layperson.*

Two white men with prison muscles and brilliantly Brilliantine'd hair waited
for the electric locks to buzz at the end of fifty minutes and entered the
classroom. S retreated to a neutral corner and looked out the window,

fascinated by a pigeon. "Mr. Hoffa has a birthday comin' up," one said. They left and returned two weeks later. "Mr. Hoffa likes Cuban cigars." A week later I said to them, "Even if I would, where could I get Cuban cigars in central Pennsylvania?" Three days later, "A nice young fella like yourself would do well to remember Mr. Hoffa's birthday." They spoke to each other as if I wasn't there. "Mr. Hoffa's birthday, four days away." I taped a six-pack of Phillies cheroots inside *The Portable Nietzsche* that the Catholic Chaplain's office had stamped. They came back in a week: "Ever think about law school? The freight could be paid. A nice young fella like yourself."

I took some "substance abuse" training with guards and FBI and other serious men in suits. The legal, psychological, sociological, medical aspects of drugs. Drugs and law enforcement. To start we saw a film about fetal drug addiction and I threw up a little in my mouth. There were lectures by police and lawyers about the production, distribution, and consumption of drugs, very lugubrious and chilling, after which I got to see and sniff various white and black and brown compounds laid out on tables like at a junior-high science fair. I learned *bonita*, poor quality heroin cut with lactose, and I learned about black tar heroin. I loved saying *black tar heroin* as much as I could in my civilian life ["Could I have a quart of orange juice and some black tar heroin?"]. I loved the *lexis* I learned in that room. *Fu, fuel, gauge, gangster, gash, giggle, grunt.* I got to smoke, well not smoke, but pass around a lit cigarette of marijuana with FBI during which there wasn't even a smirk. Don't bogart that joint, my friend. The other men looked like my college football teammates.

Text and countertext: Philip Roth in his autobiographical essay "Joe College" writes about his time at Bucknell, about the cultural schism set in motion by his exile from Jewish Newark to goyishe central Pennsylvania. I was his "Secret Sharer," his part-Jewish Joe College alter ego, injected into mainstream football/campus culture fifteen years later. Then, four years later, Joe Jail.

I knew it as "woofing," two men in the yard toe-to-toe fighting, but at a lover's distance, a boxer's distance, more of an aggressive singing—an unarmed battle to subdue your opponent by words that summoned all the caged cleverness, metaphysical conceit, repressed homoeroticism, overt homoeroticism, street wit and prison vernacular. It probably duplicated the daily condition of inmates: wanting to erupt in violence but against whom or what and with what? So woofing. This verbal fighting demanded an audience, and it wasn't over until the loser went speechless or the circle proclaimed a winner after a slander about mother fucking, hygiene, intellectual acumen, and shit eating. S called it signifying. The Muslims said, "Woofin'? That's the dozens. But we don't encourage disparaging our African-American brothers and sisters, sir." "You don't have to call me sir," I said. "It's our way to show respect for all persons."

My mother called, where was I and what and how? I was spending all my time in jail. What more could the Selective Service do to me?

I don't remember breathing, but I must have taken a breath. I remember the diving-bell pressure and oceanic noise broken by slams and howls. I don't remember the seasons, but I remember putting up the top of the car and turning the heater on giving a ride to an "inmate" who turned out to be a government informer on anti-war activities.

I never could identify the smell: ozone, mercurochrome, male oils, venison, spills of guilt [I imagined] mopped up by bleach, disinfected rage. I remember the first time I witnessed a "count": the black and brown men obediently rendering their numbers to the jailers. I was unaccountably terrified. To be white is to do the counting.

"It is the innocence which constitutes the crime." James Baldwin. They were right, the guards, those astute literary critics, about *The Fire Next Time*. It was incendiary, accusatory, true.

I remember trying to articulate the inside/outside paradigm: *Crooks outside/ Saints inside* became *Some Crooks, some Saints inside/indifferent assholes outside* became *Crooks inside so violently anti-authoritarian they won't accept help from anybody/Crooks outside so violently authoritarian that Nixon would be elected [and reelected] and the war would go on.* The only thing I was sure of was the virgules.

One student would answer only if the sum of the problem were 2, as in "Deuce, cut her loose." He answered only in rhyme, clanging. "Make that 2, Yabba Dabba Doo."

Another student showed me his scrapbook. A picture of him in a burgundy sheath, a bare-midriff piece in emerald, a red peplum with a blouse, a strapless white, *that's champagne,* gown. He told me about the tuck. And tape. But what I remember most is the photo of the family at Thanksgiving fanned out behind the bounty: turkey, stuffing, cranberry, mashed potatoes, and tax stamps proudly on all the liquor bottles. You and me.

Limitation. Success.
Galling limitation must not be persevered in.

Nine in the fifth place means:
Sweet limitation brings good fortune.
Going brings esteem.

My mother, the marine, was crying. "Sit down. Are you sitting down? You've been reclassified." The drop in the alphabet from 1-A to 1-Y meant: *Registrant available for military service, but qualified only in case of war or national emergency*. As far as she knew it went something like this: Files from my trip to West Point as a high-school football recruit and subsequent disqualification [shoulder separation] were sent to my draft board who added them to the X-rays and transcripts of injuries sustained playing college football and the draft board thought better of me as a specimen. "The US Military Academy got you out of the military," she said.

I would not have to go to war, but I would serve.

I drove around and played Miles.

It seems now a cheap, absurdly theatrical, backwards, and shitty kind of resistance. Kids my age, friends, were coming home in body bags: I wasn't oblivious to this. It wasn't just TV. A kid I had gone to school with, the skinny red-haired kid in the corner, was a gunner on a helicopter. Kids I had slammed my head into in football games were a flag folded over and over into a starry blue triangle. I wasn't any less bewildered by this outcome than I was by living out of my car and plotting escapes or self-mutilation. Or by teaching in, being in, jail.

Identity formation: Whoever I was when I had arrived [Joe College? Mr. SDS?], I was not that person now. That person had had a blanket thrown over him and was taken down. That person got cut up and bled out. I would do my time in the company of men and be released to my own recognizance. I wouldn't see white and free without seeing a boundary, a concussion, a lockdown, a count. And a black man in a jean jacket in the rain playing a saxophone against the wall, the walls holding but shaking slightly.

I left shaking slightly, being wrong, speaking a different language: prison language. The private, circumscribed, contraband smuggled in and out under the tongue, subject to punishment, woofing, capable of offending, defending, silencing, inducing a trance, whispering, breaking, signifying,

41

wall-echoed, racial, coded tribal belonging. Language capable of checking, abashing, and undoing the giant. The warden, the parole board, the Catholic chaplain spoke one [white] language; the inmates, the jazz broadcasts, the *I Ching* spoke another. Whose grammar? Whose music? Whose nation?

I got out and turned to words, "the taming power of the small." I would practice a curious puffing. I would begin my apprenticeship, a twenty-year bid. I would become a woman in the eyes of the world.

Prison narratives, captivity narratives, slave narratives, Puritan conversion narratives share similar duress, small spaces, the soul under pressure, the construction and question of the "other," hall of shame/hall of fame, the hidden coming into view, the articulation of a struggle and survival.

What I couldn't see were the fire hoses trained on S and the young black men that blasted them into Lewisburg and the snarling dogs that took bites out of them through the court system and the new black and brown plantation built to house the casualties of the early assaults of Nixon's drug war.

Most days I walk with an inmate beside me.

"Spill," S said, and I spilled.

Poetry is the spill [excess and witness].

Straight line, broken line, straight line.

MEAT

His charge was to make something out of the contracting cool
that glows and then goes vagrant, whole systems of courtships
and compensations that get lost in a letter appealing to the dust
and the red-blue extremities of stars. His charge was to make
something out of the over/understory or ignore the clot
and throw off the scent of the creatures who would find him.
He bypassed the red morning to get to the blue hours
of towering occupation. He ignored the war, those signatures
and sutures. He saw an animal. He saw an exceptional
animal in a small space where capture became data
for the glorious self, where contingency became pity.
His animals had wings, no predicament of meat, no maggot
on the carcass, nothing slit or skinned into oblivion. He felt
no crisis in the ugly open mouth. He never saw an eyelash
viper, a dung beetle, a slug, let alone a side of beef. He never saw
a woman with lice. He arrowed into a century as if it were an eternity
[the woman with lice there with her scratches], but he could not
follow the arc back to the suffering moment at the start
when the cow got captive bolted by the sky god. His agony
was archery: fletching and a taut string pinched by two fingers
launched into the distance he loved. Distance and velocity
moved him and moved him into beyond [nowhere
Zen New Jersey]. Non-bodied sky, circus tricks [acrobats,
animals in small spaces] and the question does it stick its shaft into
something or nothing? Splendid something [Saint Sebastian]
or miserable, lice-ridden nothing? It seems a reasonable question
language can't answer with its hypnosis, its horizon.
Was it an immanent thing or the sensation of holding the immediate,
then the terrible release? For all the shooting into the blue

he never accounted for the poxed, the poor, anyone's daughter,
the slave, the baited and bashed. His suffering was sensational,
angel-ridden, and violent without the fact and for this reason
I do him in—the brooder, the moocher of beauty—after first subduing
him, because that's what we do in my country. For all the arrows
he let go, not one struck a wallah with one leg who lives between
the tracks with his wife and kids. He killed, this smug archer,
this Sagittarius, his family and got away with it by becoming subtle
and expansive and the veins of his skin showed through.
I want him and that part of me that loves courting the blue
and the breezes to be harmed, but beautifully, as we do in my country.

RUN

The worldspeak goes in one direction telling its sad tale
and the song, before a note or two are even heard—
like a particle emoting from a wave—pushes the sadness aside
and makes an ache for something else and then the song gets
enslaved to the ongoing process of master this, master that
so no more singing. And no to your freestyle with beatbox
and flexing. No to your jazz flute. But you heard something,
didn't you? What was it you heard? The crack of the winterkill
or the car alarms busting June's honeymoon or your name
from the dream radio. You love the either/or and the implied lips
and incomprehensible ear. We all know the story of your beauty
and the cuts down to size you made to multiply, glorify. Afterward
you could hear the fire, the fugitive particles, the panic of the rich.
After the cuts you saw only infrared, two dimensions, mirrors,
and your mouth. Who is going to sing about it now, dear one?
There are new territories, new pronouns, new accounts, new veils.
Some come in your color: your ghost, your smoke. The I/you
is always a busted engine. It's never just you, sweetness.
[The teacher said avoid *always* and *never*.] Once I found you
in a corridor and pushed you gently up against the wall and shut
your gratified/gratifying mouth with my mouth. None of that happened
as prelude to the nothing that would become of us. I got broke.
You got to be compounded. I got different. You were able to bear
and bull your way out. I went into corridors and erasures of my class.
[The teacher said X minus Y equals what?] You got to visit in dream
the torn forms of the self. There's a song for this. We all know the song.
At least there's a voice and a burden and a surrender. But no singer.
Before the future the heart got pressed into the service of the mouth,
and you wonder why the songs were always grateful to the master.

45

The heart is still useful when the plane crashes. It's the muscle
the linebacker needs to shed the tackle and deliver the hit. Or
it's the muscle you need to pump the chemicals to shed
the placenta and deliver the kid. In the heart nothing takes root.
[Roots need historical dark, a gulag, a middle passage.]
Yours lives in desert sun, thriving with fire ants, scorpions,
and sunsets. A slave song: *You gotta escape for your life,*
bright angels above and the chorus: *Oh run, run, mourner run.*

BOILERMAKER

I stopped drinking [anything] because I didn't want the stall
in the present, the alibi of the why wherefore. The amber-colored
life with foam [like a demon, like an ocean] was no longer a way to be
god or girl. The red/white life in tulip glasses, the doubled, poured,
spilled life in neon dark was no longer a way to work out the emergence,
the pretext, the other thing [outstream, influx] that wants a mind/
body to be angelic but not wasted, arrogant, adult. [Not crashed,
lit up, beery. Not buzzed, boiled, loopy.] I was not above an apology
or below buying an indulgence if someone was selling a piece of the cross.
Goodbye to the low flame and the cold sleep. Goodbye to society
and my Roundtable, where I would send further regrets
for slurs I uttered when I wanted wit. I would listen for the curious
puffing, the rhymes and off-rhymes [hips, lips, nipples], but
still wanted more [hunger: see Billie Holiday, see Simone Weil].
There was nothing between me and the source world that speaks
in rat language, spirit dispirited, nature denatured, mute in the back
room where there's a thing in a cage, where there are no terms
or excuses, where all is elegy, but you are cared for and the dark
dies a Macbeth death and the tongue cut out of terror
that spoke to you the way the Hutu spoke to the Tutsi,
the way the brooch spoke to the eye, and the shattered
glass spoke to the wrist. The limb grows back, the lizard puffs
its throat. I could be the weapon. I could be the rain. I could be
the children, the names of the children, the names of the weapons,
the ponds filled with silver, slivers of glass, teeth and the hair,
the eyelash, the names and the Caravaggio dark, thrown down
in shadow, bent back by storm, torn, the names of the children.

BIRD

I lived between the hemisphere of songbirds and the hemisphere
of men. The birds kept their necessary distance and the men
their self-consciousness, their standing thereness. The things
men loved died and they were inconsolable, except by force.
It was impossible to say for whose sake they were tortured.
When one came home in a big black bag, other men would lift him,
a kind of cannibalism, but there was no him, apparently,
although they continued to use the words *glory, honor, vision.*
[The last a bird term.] They continued to use bandages, to look
elsewhere, to be contorted into postures of wake or suspend
belief, but for whose sake and for what furthering?
It was a winner-take-all system in the hemisphere, summer
or winter. [Some say the songbirds were subtitles, some say décor,
some say there was some subversion in the call.] Men continued
to prefer, to urge to their advantage, add options to the standard,
gather onlookers. They snowballed. They boiled. They detailed.
They spilled. They wasted with such skill they called it
ours, our way of life. Men blocked the exits, confused the hemispheres
with mirrors, windows, and the mix of optimism and emptiness
the songbirds found holes in. One song was *exit, exit,* one song was
por favor. Men muscled under. Men had ten men inside them,
which explains their skin, and ten men [boys] enlisted, which explains
the embargo on joy, the ravishing angelic toys, faces, recognitions.
I suppose it all comes down to the discolored dusk and a walk
around the heart-shaped lake where men behave like
recreated birds, mate, splash in the thisness, the whatness of puddles,
flash the colors. I haven't said much about the other hemisphere,
which I only know in bits I don't understand [man term],

but who has the music, I ask? Who needs the cuts to enter the world?
Who needs no market? Who knows no handedness, pity, or duty?
Who brought the mail from Tunis, and who knows where the ark should land?

SISTER

Boy sucks the xylem out of Ben Franklin's system and the stinking
ginkgoes and sycamores of anarchic, hamstrung parks and lived rich
[but poor] everywhere in Ur, everywhere in the evaporating
European theater, African summer of the 1100 block [rent
share, Quonset hut], shock of feeding with one eye and dying
in the other. Boy ate ten times his boy weight each day and at night
sucked out the juice from the telephone, gas, and electric,
which flourished as billet-doux in the kitchen where the big cats
killed the antelope, one eye eating seeds, one eye dying
as he was seized by the talon of an F-18 Falcon. [He made that up.
The lie gave him short flight not the bulk of the left/right halves
of the badly-glued fuselage.] There was a wobble in the differential,
a noise from the secreting transmission of the Ford. He bore
deeper into the silence where the dead sister lived
like a glass-boxed princess of empty that could not be filled
by butter or regular. One eye saw the crib, one eye saw the supper.
One saw the trembling intervals. Toy box, icebox, weep hole, locker.
Bread- and strongbox, popsicle jewel box, soldered tool, vanity, knot
in the knothole fell out of the wall, but nothing could hold her
measured breath. In cellar, in drain, in ditch Her. The tar bars,
potholes, tremors in the car the boy ciphered. [One eye
phone pole sunk in creosote, one eye on the horizon.]
He could not overturn the numbers turning over on the dash
like eyes rolling up in the skull, zero, zero, zero sister.
One eye saw river, one eye saw rigor. One eye saw thrill ride,
one eye saw kill void. Outside the car window was rush or still
depending on his looking near or far: broods, heat shimmers,
rain. I miss her. The dead sister was a lie
to move him from there to here.

BUTTON

I did it and did it and then I didn't do it anymore, but like a dry
drunk I kept wanting the wanting to prefigure the loss, an end
of the wanting, maybe, or a rescue of the wanting from more wanting
so I lugged the body up as many floors it took for it to be
subtle. I counted the buttons. I reread the letters. I became 65,
then 66 percent consolation, the rest light I could no longer clearly see.
I became a folded form, but a form 65 percent in parenthesis [an old
man in his tights who leads the mummers into town playing
his accordion]. The Party wanted me, then they wanted me
gone, then they wanted me got. There was a freewheeling need
to repeat the same five bars and four beats, no cheating.
There was a need to drop down and do it and do it. At night
when I couldn't sleep I would push the buttons through the holes
and so undo and so be undone. I remember a lilac one
[I can't remember the want], and a big stars-and-stripes one.
Buttons were flat faces with strangely empathetic dark eyes, faces
of bone, faces of shell I'd thumb and finger until I was still, counting,
touching, pushing the disk through the slit like the tip of the tongue
against the teeth. [I know you, reader, came secretly into my city
and replaced my books with inferior identical copies.
You should know, reader, I have the real copies here and keep
other copies of those copies in the ten duplicate cities I wander among.]
I was never the quick-change artist but took time to fold back the fabric
and push the little planetary plates through. The buttons had two
[I prefer four] identical holes in them, dark spots like lunar seas
[sea of nectar, sea of serenity]. The sadness is part of this
[the Party wanted angry not sad], the serial release, the buttons
letting go of their grasp of the shirt, the skirt, the skin and then summer—
plenty of glistening things, flies with their multiplying eyes, revolution

flourishing in ten Arab cities and here where the hydrants are uncapped
and spray fractals over the exorbitant children with dark eyes
in the river god's custody [sea of fecundity] and serves them Kool-Aid,
duplicating fruit [drupelets of black and raspberry]. These acts soothe
me as do the many mute stones of the cherries [don't tell me, reader,
the world is an argument]. In one of my cities I'm satisfied, in nine
I'm anxious because I sense it could be otherwise. [Reader,
how could you do this to me? Reader, are you a member of the Party?]
In Baghdad I'm in Cairo. In Cairo I'm in Illinois [with anarchic Huck].
In Rome I'm in New York fingering the buttons and here
I'm doing something then doing something to that
so I'm not demonized by the wanting while I'm doing it.

POLLEN

The vulture rides the thermals to identify a knacker. The bee
finds me with his hind legs in harem pants of pollen. He hovers.
He's absolutely still. He's furiously moving. Undisturbed by paradox—
miniature Heraclitus. I'm already picked clean except for color
[infrared] and anger [and accidents]. Then he's on his way to further
the planet. I'm on my way to be still yet the still breathing thing
the vulture circles. I'm crossed by his shadow. Twenty-five years growing,
twenty-five years living, twenty-five years of unpollinated dying. Pick me clean
of my melancholy [which prevented me from furthering the planet].
You'll have to accept the black bile as well as the sweet fat under
the ribs and my explicitness, my wish fulfilled, my hits and misses
with the claw hammer and the prodigious calculations
that distinguish my species. In addition, my additions, my specifics
[my attention to line items, my methyl isocyanate, the infinitesimal
print in the documents from Bhopal]. And there are my police
when I need them [exquisite spit and polish of my carabinieri uniform].
Plus the need-to-know basis of my failures, the Rupert Murdoch
broadcasts of my triumphs. Now, I'm asked only to promise
it won't happen anymore, to be visited, or to be used
beautifully by the vultures with their surgically-scrubbed heads.
In fact, I'm not asked as I had imagined. In fact the facts were determined
by dream [flying carpets, harems, children inhaling concentrations
of chemicals] in the hammock I thought was determination.
I could be the stuff for honey. I could be [will be] summoned
by the gullet of the wind or be ground, water, milk.

HONEY

Why couldn't he shut his eyes and be the thin continuum
and sleep and not thrash about for as long as it takes to equalize
the ratio of terror to pleasure? He sees the fetus in the light bulb
[his baby, coiled animal, eye]—light that could signal the arrival
of the paramours or enthrall a moth. Why couldn't his sense of time
as sensuous intuition remain unscathed and a body-based system
of continuance, sad in proportions of hubris to music, carry him
in the betweenness? What business of his was the affliction? What
business was his? Why couldn't the fluency be between the note and
the echo? Fluency [lack] was the affliction. He had to have silence
or bring on the drum kit: snare, hi-hat, splash cymbal, ride. Dark
matter surrounds the baby in the light bulb, but dark matter mostly
surrounds us all, and still we have our facts. Facts were the affliction.
Let him take as long as it takes to assemble the unknowable stories—
that's what poetry is for—out of memos, microphones, and a system
of numbered pulleys. Let him place the trophies, the free weights,
the test tubes, and the beakers [like displays of things seized
by the authorities] along the base of the walls of the underground
bunker. Is he [it reads sadly masculine] fugitive? Or sad?
Passive-aggressive, photophobic, or Proust? Is the only way
out of this art that wrestles angels or *cops into alleys . . . taking their weapons*
as Baraka said [and then what then what with men and their weapons]?
Then what is the affliction. Or is he [the incubus, the disease] at work
in his leisure in the secret reordering in the measure of Dickinson's
misery to ecstasy: *the body so cold no fire can warm*? It takes some continuum.
It's not just frame, frame, frame and then a machine that dispenses stickiness.
It helps to be neither he nor she but someone with the affliction who imagines
being: taking the cache of honey found in the cemetery to downtown
in bottles and offering it for sale. It takes some stolen honey that is good

for embalming and dressing the wounds of the West. [It's the perishable
that won't perish over time]. Shut your eyes. Move away from the window.
Move away from the mirror. Move away from him, her. Let go
of all that you can [trees, ideas, the nail gun, the baby]. Let the fingers
be free for counting the things that move beyond [between] your ability
to count, move faster than the frames of the birth [of a Nation], the death
[of a Salesman]: that twin bill the bulb projects [and the moth batters].
It's not start, cut, cold. It's more like plunder, honey, fade
into the fading business, music, lights up, cold, and the continuing.

TRUE/FALSE

Or maybe a third thing neither bewildered nor banal nor noble. Nobody
ever said noble. Neither horrific [Is this wire connected to the current
connected to the genitals of Rumsfeld and al-Jamadi?] nor decent. No blood
let, no clot. Not infliction. Not vehicle for the blithe spirit. No dump
of facts, tears. A third thing. Not solution [God, assisted suicide, space],
not problem [sadness, violence, your face]. I worked hard to make a third thing,
a lot of it was working hard for men. They loved me nice. They loved me
pink, but I didn't draw an audience. I sold maybe negative thirty tickets
to the dance. They loved me as sexy governess, bending over, kneeling,
but not as Antigone, her arms stretched out in the whirlwind in the desert,
tangled and sweaty. I got paid for my agonies,
my essences. I preferred the amber and rose of Tabu. I was wrong
about the third thing. It is bewildered, bewildering, horrific, cheap,
a problem that came not in twos but in battalions [with over thirty rounds
in the clip]. I wanted to be governed since I did the violence anyway,
without agency. I did it innocently. I wanted to be told [scolded,
clipped, cored] what I could bite and kiss, say and feel, and what
would be permitted. Tell me to look at the Yule log burning on TV
or tell me to look away. Tell me what to feel about the camera
and the fake blood. What sound to make in the mosque or out.
I was wrong about the vehicle and the feeling and agonies
connected to me connected to my essence spilling out
into the country [outside the city, on the reservation, outside
the jurisdiction, into the desert where my Antigone is buried], leaking
out half and quarter lives from corroded barrels like notes
that get agonized over time by some treaty with wind [with emptiness,
with lead] and make the unruly tune you hear in the night:
it's ghosts bossing you to look at their wounds,
their ugly burns and in/out holes. It's raccoons.

FERMENT

I saw the body of the jackfruit fall. I saw the body of the hero
fall, *his armor clanging on his body*. Then the juice and sutras
of the little spell of emptiness or the greater discourse of seed
and ovary. I saw the place ransacked to find a substitute
for the succulents—the lychee, the peach, the flower
infolded in the fig—that give up their season, their nation
[mango, American pumpkin], the famous fated beauty/terror
rift before the swoon of the future. I saw that luscious rot.
I saw first thieves then police toss that place. I loved
that part. This is the farewell, the flailing without the salt.
This is the brood in place of a bowl of fruit, the fret
in place of a hero's rage in his tent before he remembers
to sleep, eat, regret. I saw how the light scratches into all
the surfaces, how the air agitates. Then the virtuoso work
of the one-celled begins to mortify and multiply the world,
as if it were doing nothing, so much done by doing nothing.
I live in a sorrow culture, a pleasure culture, a culture frothy
with grievance, yeasty with nostalgia. I live in a prewar,
postwar culture where what is written is pulped and vectored
like a virus. Ashen light, clouds of sulfuric acid, signatures
of lightning: this could be the planet Venus where love is
adored and scorned, life is sentimental, life is 400 dollars
or more. It froths. It foams like a god in the ocean.
On this planet I saw flights of sparrows and hooded crows.
There's gratuitous beauty, unwarranted, immoderate beauty
as an agent to oblivion. This blue, this curvature, this Rome—
a further way to forgo. Because no one else will, reader,
remember the things spirited away. Remember those hustling,
those surrendered, those breathing then not. The spectacle

makes us forget. I forgot the shape and color of the cup
and the teargas canister. I forgot about the occupation
and the trail of tears when I saw the sea's glint
and green muscly swells. Beholding is a kind of blindness.
History smells as the body becomes a bubbling god.
What separates the curds and whey? What allows me
to enter the room, through the small door, where
we can have this difficult conversation?

INDEX

Abdul-Jabbar, Aquanetta, Amadou Diallo, Antigone
aid and abetting, arias, art
and, and, and

Baghdad, Bhopal, betweenness, Big House,
Baldwin [James], Bonhoeffer [Dietrich], Brown [James]
bees, bombers [*see* lambs]

Cage [John], College [Joe], Coltrane
Caravaggio, Cleaver [Eldridge], Conrad
capitalism, childhood, corridos

Democratic National Convention, Dickinson
dark matter, disobedient

ecstatic, erode, excess

Fanon [Frantz], Franklin [Ben]
Fort Dix
face, field hollers, funnel clouds, fubar
flayed things

Ghost Dance, Gaye [Marvin], Genet [Jean]
gauge, gangster, gash, giggle

Hamlet's father, Heraclitus, Holiday [Billie], Huck
Hoffa [Jimmy], Heartbreak Ridge
honey, Honey Bun

I Ching, iffy, indebtedness

Joyce, Judas, Jung

Kant, Kansas, Koran
Kabuki, kudzu

lambs [*see* bombers], law [*see* storm]
Lao Tzu, Leary [Timothy]

Macbeth, Magic, Mao, Moses, *Muhammad Speaks*
maggot, mandatory minimum, meat
money

necessary, need-to-know
Nowhere Zen New Jersey

Oklahoma, Onondaga, Oz

passive-aggressive
pollen, protection racket, putto
pomegranate, prophet
Paley [Grace], Pope [Alexander], Proust

question, question
quid pro quo, Queen City, quit [one hit and]

raga, rag
root systems, ruin
Rama Lama, Reagan, Reed [Lou], Rumsfeld

Simone [Nina], Sinatra [Frank]
storm [*see* law]
Saint Sebastian, Shelley, Sioux, Sun Ra,

spill,
shepherds, sitar, surrender

Taming Power of the Small
Troy, Tupelo, Tunis, Tuscaloosa
Twickenham
tú

usted
unauthorized, unnumbered
Ur

vamp
viper [eyelash]

Wallace [George], White [Mrs.], Wilde [Oscar]
wallah
white project, white noise, witness

x, X [Malcolm], X

Yankee, yabba dabba doo, Y

Zion [*see* Little Zion Tabernacle Church]